GEOGRAPHY OF THE WORLD

THE TIMEWORN

URALS

By Barbara A. Somervill

THE CHILD'S WORLD®
CHANHASSEN, MINNESOTA

The Child's World

Published in the United States of America by The Child's World®
PO Box 326, Chanhassen, MN 55317-0326
800-599-READ
www.childsworld.com

Content Adviser:

Mark Williams,

Associate Professor,

University of Colorado,

Boulder, Colorado

Photo Credits: Cover/frontispiece: TASS/Sovfoto.
Interior: Bryan & Cherry Alexander: 18; Animals Animals/Earth Scenes: 9 (OSF/O.
Newman), 14 (Bradley W. Stahl), 17 (Darek Kapp); Corbis: 11 (Steve Raymer), 26
(Dave G. Houser); Wolfgang Kaehler: 6; Wolfgang Kaehler/Corbis: 8, 16, 21; Jacques
Langevin/Corbis Sygma: 22; Novosti/Sovfoto: 4, 24; TASS/Sovfoto: 5, 12, 13.

The Child's World®: Mary Berendes, Publishing Director

Editorial Directions, Inc.: E. Russell Primm, Editorial Director; Melissa McDaniel,
Line Editor; Katie Marsico, Associate Editor; Judi Shiffer, Associate Editor and Library
Media Specialist; Matthew Messbarger, Editorial Assistant; Susan Hindman, Copy
Editor; Sarah E. De Capua and Lucia Raatma, Proofreaders; Marsha Bonnoit, Peter
Garnham, Terry Johnson, Olivia Nellums, Chris Simms, Katherine Trickle, and
Stephen Carl Wender, Fact Checkers; Tim Griffin/IndexServ, Indexer; Cian Loughlin
O'Day, Photo Researcher; Linda S. Koutris, Photo Selector; XNR Productions, Inc.,
Cartographer

The Design Lab: Kathleen Petelinsek, Design and Page Production

Library of Congress Cataloging-in-Publication Data
Somervill, Barbara A.
  The timeworn Urals / by Barbara A. Somervill.
    p. cm. — (Geography of the world)
  Includes index.
  ISBN 1-59296-335-8 (lib. bdg. : alk. paper) 1. Ural Mountains Region (Russia)—
Juvenile literature. I. Title. II. Geography of the world series.
  DK511.U7S6 2004
  914.7'43—dc22   2004003832

TABLE OF CONTENTS

CHAPTER ONE

THE BUZZING OF BEES

I n the Shulgan-Tash Preserve in the Southern Ural Mountains, the linden trees are abuzz with activity. The bustle comes from wild Burzyan honeybees. These bees are very rare. They produce some of the sweetest honey in the world.

The best way to reach Shulgan Tash Preserve's remote regions is on horseback.

There are few treats sweeter than honey from Burzyan bees.

In the Ural Mountains that divide Europe from Asia, people have been collecting honey from Burzyan honeybees for more than 800 years. Today, ranger-beekeepers in Shulgan-Tash collect honey much the way their ancestors did. They carve hollow hives in linden trees to attract the bees. Then, like the local brown bears, the rangers climb the trees to collect the delicious "gold" from Burzyan hives. In the timeworn Urals, some things never change.

CHAPTER TWO

THE MAKING OF A
MOUNTAIN RANGE

Changing the earth's surface is a slow process. Mountain building

may take a million years. In the history of earth, that is not long.

It is not surprising, then, that a mountain range such as the Urals

could be 250 million years old.

Thick pine forests cover much of the Urals.

Mountains are built in several different ways. Volcanoes, earthquakes, incredible pressure, and massive collisions can all build mountains.

The Ural Mountains resulted from a huge collision. The outer layer of the earth is called the crust. Earth's crust is like a broken eggshell. It has cracks and cuts. The cracks divide the crust into giant pieces called plates. Earth has about 20 different plates. Some plates are continents, and some make up the seafloor.

When two continents crash together, they build mountains. The land where they collide is bent, twisted, folded, and uplifted. Jagged peaks rise above deep valleys and narrow gorges. The Ural Mountains were built when the European and Asian plates smashed into each other.

As mountains go, the Urals are short and stumpy. No peaks rise above 6,500 feet (2,000 meters). Wind, weather, and water have eroded the Urals until their peaks no longer soar above the clouds. The Urals are timeworn. They have earned the nickname the Gray-Haired Mountains.

Mountain ranges support a variety of **ecosystems.** The Urals include grass-covered **steppes,** tree-covered **taiga,** and barren Arctic **tundra.**

The steppe is dry, cold grassland. In the Urals, steppes are found in Kazakhstan and southern Russia. Grasses in the steppes can range in height from about 18 inches to 54 inches (46 centimeters to 137 cm). Many

Gentle, rolling steppes provide pastures for horses and cattle.

steppe animals, such as squirrel-like susliks, burrow underground.

Taiga is Russian for "forest." In the Urals, taiga lies between the tundra and the steppe. Pine, cedar, larch, spruce, and aspen grow in the taiga. Weasels and badgers feed on

Arctic foxes are opportunistic feeders. This means they hunt anything they can eat.

ground squirrels and meadow voles. Songbirds nest in the trees each spring. They feed their chicks insects, berries, and seeds.

To the north, the Arctic tundra lies cold and forbidding. Ice fields stretch like fingers between low-lying mountains. The tundra supports no trees. Its plants hug close to the ground. Caribou browse on gray-green lichens. Sleek Arctic foxes hunt Ob lemming against a stark white background.

Scientists learn how mountains formed by looking at the rocks that make up the mountains. The region where the Urals are now was once a giant sea. Over time, sand, clay, and skeletons of sea creatures collected on the seafloor. Water and gravity pressed down on this material, slowly turning it into **sedimentary** rocks, such as sandstone and limestone.

Sedimentary rock is not very hard. Running water can easily wear it away to carve out caves. Limestone caves are found all over the Ural Mountains.

Over a long period of time, pressure and heat can change sedimentary rock into **metamorphic** rock. In the Southern Urals, layers of metamorphic rock are up to 4 miles (6.5 km) deep.

The Ural Mountains contain rich mineral deposits. The region has plentiful supplies of gold, iron, copper, nickel, silver, zinc, and cobalt. Gems such as sapphires, emeralds, topazes, aquamarines, amethysts, and garnets are also mined in the Urals.

CHAPTER THREE

ABOUT THE URALS

The Ural Mountains run north and south, stretching from the Arctic Ocean all the way to the Mugodzhar Hills in northwestern Kazakhstan. Though the Urals divide Europe from Asia, they pass through only two countries: Russia and Kazakhstan. To the west of the Urals are the great cities of Russia: Saint Petersburg and Moscow. To the east lie the bleak, forbidding lands of Siberia.

Russia's major cities, such as Saint Petersburg, lie far to the west of the Ural Mountains.

The Ural Mountain range runs for about 1,500 miles (2,400 km).

The width of the Urals varies up to 200 miles (322 km). The range

has four main divisions: Southern, Middle, Northern, and Polar.

The Southern Urals lie in south-central Russia and a small section

A map of the Urals

of northern Kazakhstan. This region features low-lying mountains, dense forests, and broad pastures. The foothills are covered with steppe. Major cities in the Southern Urals include Nizhniy Tagil, Yekaterinburg, Chelyabinsk, and Magnitogorsk.

Cities in the Urals have an interesting mixture of old architecture and modern skyscrapers.

The Middle Urals are covered with pine forests, deep ravines, and fertile valleys. The cities of Krasnoturinsk and Severouralsk mark the southern boundary of this region.

The Northern Urals consist of a narrow strip of mountains. Few trees, craggy peaks, and tight valleys paint a gloomy landscape. Gora Narodnaya, the highest peak in the Ural Mountains, rises 6,214 feet (1,894 m) in the Northern Urals.

The Polar Urals stretch from the Arctic Circle north to the Kara

Sea. The mountains here are covered with tundra. Bitter cold winds whip across the treeless plains during the long winters. Moss, lichen, and sedge hug the ground to protect themselves from the weather. Many tundra animals are summer visitors only. This includes the millions of ducks, geese, and swans that nest in the Polar Urals each year. Other animals, such as Ob lemmings and ground squirrels, sleep away the long winter months.

Dozens of rivers cut through the Ural Mountains. Most drain

Tundra plants cluster close to the ground for protection from bitter winter winds.

north into the Arctic Ocean or west into the Caspian Sea. On the Urals' eastern slopes, the Tobol, Iset, Severnaya, and Tura rivers are **tributaries** of the Ob River. The Ob then pours into the Kara Sea, which opens into the Arctic Ocean. The Pechora River and its tributaries,

including the Ilych, the Usa, and the Shchugor, are on the Urals' western slopes. They head to the Barents Sea. Northern rivers are usually frozen for more than half the year.

In the south, the Kama and Ural rivers drain the land east of the Caspian Sea. The Belaya and Vishera rivers feed into the Kama, while the Sakmara empties into the Ural River.

Lakes dot the eastern slopes of the Urals. The largest are the Uvildy, Itkul, Turgoyak, and Tavatuy. These lakes all lie in the Southern and Middle Urals. In the Arctic region, Lake Bolshoye Shchuchye is the deepest. Ice covers this lake for most of the year.

CHAPTER FOUR

PLANTS AND ANIMALS
OF THE URALS

Many different plants and animals live in the Ural Mountains. The three main ecosystems in the Urals—steppe, taiga, and tundra—each support different kinds of plants and animals.

Wild grasses and wildflowers cover the steppes on the Southern Urals' eastern slopes. In the summer, oxeye daisies and yellow bedstraw flash against the pale green of wild grasses. Small animals such

Fireweed turns summer meadows into flaming swatches of red.

as susliks, jerboas, and mice thrive in the steppes. Grass snakes and common adders slither through rustling grasses.

Taiga forests support a mix of creatures. Tawny owls, Scops owls, kestrels, and carrion crows swoop down from their nests to catch scurrying rodents. Siberian chipmunks

Owls keep an eye out for small rodents in the forests of the Urals.

and black woodpeckers make their homes in downed tree trunks. Some 4,000 brown bears feast on forest berries, nuts, and roots. Playful otters glide through the taiga's rivers, while moose graze on riverside grasses. Root voles build homes hidden below willow thickets. Eurasian dippers and northern shovelers nest near rushing rivers. Deep beneath the larch, oak, and birches, black-and-red capercaillies dance to attract mates.

The Arctic tundra looks barren under heavy winter snows. But spring thaws bring the land to life. The tundra landscape blends spongy marshes, shallow lakes, icy rivers, and gentle rises. The tundra supports millions of ducks, swans, and geese each summer. Sables, martens, ermines, and Siberian weasels steal eggs from nests during the summer months. During the rest of the year, these creatures hunt rats, voles, shrews, hares, and dormice.

CARIBOU OR REINDEER?
Caribou look just like reindeer. There's a good reason for this. They are the same species. Caribou live in the wild. Reindeer are simply caribou that live in herds owned by humans.

Caribou follow the same trails to feeding grounds each year.

Elk, moose, and caribou graze on tundra lichen, moss, and sedge.

Summer wildflowers paint a rainbow of colors on the tundra. Dainty pink rosebay and vivid rose-hued fireweed dance in the tundra winds. Arctic lupines add a splash of deep blue. White Arctic poppies and purplish marsh violets bring more colors to the landscape.

More than 200 Russian national parks protect nature in the Ural Mountains. In the south, Shulgan-Tash Zapovednik supports bears and badgers, otters and owls, hedgehogs and honeybees. Nearly 200 bird species nest in Shulgan-Tash. In the north, Yugyd-Va National Park and Pechora-Ilych Reserve maintain the vast, untouched taiga. In this region, 230 bird species, 49 mammal species, and an array of trees and wildflowers flourish. Rare species living in Yugyd-Va include golden eagles, Arctic falcons, white-tailed eagles, and peregrine falcons.

CHAPTER FIVE

THE PEOPLE OF THE URALS

Early human beings lived in Siberia, east of the Urals, more than 300,000 years ago. Those early people were hunter-gatherers. They hunted large animals and collected fruits, nuts, and roots to eat. The people moved from place to place to find new game.

The lifestyle of these people remained the same for thousands of years. Then, about 10,000 years ago, large game became scarce in Siberia. Hunting and gathering no longer provided a regular food supply. The people needed to find a more reliable source of food. They began farming.

By 8,000 B.C., people in the Urals were growing wheat, rice, oats, millet, and barley. Farmers needed to live near their fields, so they built more permanent homes. Clusters of homes formed villages. Between 5000 and 3000 B.C., humans began using metal to make knives and other tools. They tended their crops and herded animals along the Urals' western slopes and steppes.

For many centuries, the people of the Urals lived isolated lives. Then, in the early 1100s, the Russians from the west discovered that the Urals were filled with fur-bearing animals. Hunters and trappers began venturing into the Urals. By the mid-1500s, small groups of Russian settlers dotted the mountains. Settlers built Verkhoturye, the first true city in the Urals, in 1598.

The Urals have a proud farming heritage that stretches back hundreds of years.

The Urals offered broad, fertile valleys for farming. Plentiful deer, elk, moose, geese, and ducks fed settlers. Rich mineral deposits encouraged mining. By the 1630s, the region's first ironworks had been established. Between

Some people living in the Urals today are the distant relatives of the early native peoples in the Urals. They can trace their heritage back to before the Russians arrived in the area. These people include the Nenets, Komi, Mansi, Khanty, Bashkir, and Kazaks. The Nenets are related to early Siberian tribes. The Komi, Mansi, and Khanty live in the Northern and Middle Urals. They hunt, fish, and raise reindeer. The Bashkir are found in the Southern Urals. Bashkirs are famous horse breeders. Kazaks live in the lower Urals of Kazakhstan.

1700 and 1850, the Urals produced most of Russia's iron.

During the 1900s, the Russian people rebelled against their leader, Czar Nicholas II. During the revolution, the czar and his family were taken to Yekaterinburg, in the Southern Urals. There, they were murdered and buried.

Herding reindeer is a chilly family business for the Nenet people.

A new Russia emerged. This Russia was a **communist** country. Almost overnight, the communist government changed the Urals into an industrial center.

In 1924, the communist government of Russia joined together with other states in eastern Europe and central Asia to form a new country called the Soviet Union. The Soviet Union broke apart in 1991, and Russia and Kazakhstan became independent nations once again.

Today, 80 percent of the people who live in the Urals are Russian. Kazaks, Bashkirs, Nenets, and other native peoples account for only 20 percent.

The economy in the Urals is now a mix of mining, manufacturing, and farming. Mining provides many jobs in the region. Miners dig coal, lead, and iron ore. Every part of the Urals has active mining operations—even the Arctic. Oil and coal are found in the far north. To the south are gold, tungsten, nickel, and copper mines. The Middle Urals provide coal and manganese. The dense forests in the

Urals also support a timber industry.

Yekaterinburg and Chelyabinsk are the major industrial centers in the Urals. Each of these cities is home to more than 1 million peo-ple. In both of these cities, huge furnaces change raw

Factory smoke fills the air in cities such as Yekaterinburg and Chelyabinsk.

ore into iron and steel. Factories in the Urals produce equipment for gas and oil drilling and farming. They also churn out aircraft engines, telephones, and electronic equipment.

Farming remains an important part of the economy in the valleys and steppes. Dairy farms and cattle ranches dot the foothills of the Urals. Millet, wheat, and cattle feed are major crops. Farms also pro-duce potatoes, carrots, onions, beets, and cabbages.

CHAPTER SIX

THE CULTURE OF THE URALS

In the Urals, ancient cultures meet the modern-day world. Some native tribes in the Urals follow centuries-old traditions. Their music and art reflect their ancient heritage. At the same time, movies, television, and the Internet connect the Gray-Haired Mountains to the modern world.

Education is important to the people of the Urals. Children go to school from ages 7 to 17. There are also several universities and technical schools for higher learning.

Cities in the Urals offer similar events to American cities. Popular sports include hockey, skating, and soccer. Television and radio stations broadcast from Yekaterinburg and Chelyabinsk. People often go out to shopping centers, restaurants, libraries, and parks.

Music in the Urals ranges from symphony orchestras and operas to disco nightclubs and hard rock bands. Native cultures of the Urals enjoy traditional folksongs and poems. A strum on the balalaika—a type of guitar—and the Bashkirs of the Southern Urals burst into song.

Under communism, practicing religion was frowned upon. Yet the cities in the Urals have some of the most beautiful churches and cathedrals in Russia. Since communism ended in Russia in the 1990s, the people of the Urals are again filling these remarkable churches.

Easter is one of the most popular holidays in the Urals. Russians celebrate Easter by making elaborately decorated eggs and by eating kulich and paskha. Kulich is a sweet bread full of raisins, almonds, and candied fruit. Paskha is a sweet cheese dish with fruit, nuts, and vanilla flavoring.

The music of the balalaika sets toes tapping and hearts soaring.

At Christmastime, families in the Urals gather to feast on traditional foods. On Christmas Eve, 12 different dishes are served. These dishes represent the 12 apostles whom Jesus sent out to spread his beliefs. Kutya, a thick porridge made with grains, honey, and poppy seeds, plays a central role on the table. Kutya represents hope, happiness, and peace.

THE NIGHTINGALE

The Bashkirs have many folk songs about their native land. "The Nightingale" is one of them:

Sing, you lad, with all your might,
Send the air a-ringing.
Oh, the nightingale,
Where does the nightingale sing?
In the meadows it sings, by the riverside.
Let the songs that come from within
The young heart,
Send a thrill of delight and inspire
The sons of the Ural land.
Oh, the nightingale
Where does the nightingale sing?
In the meadows it sings, by the riverside.

Russian food is healthy and hearty. Russians eat rye, millet, oats, and barley in bread, beer, or as a side dish. Turnips, cabbages, cucumbers, and beets are served in salads, soups, and stews. When bitter winter winds blow, families in the Urals gather to break bread and share a bowl of stew. In the cold of the mountains, hearty fare feeds the body and keeps spirits high.

Glossary

communist (KOM-yuh-nist)
Communist refers to a system in which the government owns most businesses and controls the economy. Russia became communist after a revolution in 1917.

ecosystems (EE-koh-siss-tuhmz) Ecosystems are communities of plants, animals, water, and soil that are located in one area and that work together as a unit. The Urals support a variety of ecosystems.

metamorphic (met-uh-MOR-fik) A metamorphic rock is a type of rock formed by high heat and pressure. Gneiss and schist are two types of metamorphic rock.

sedimentary (sed-uh-MEN-tuh-ree) Sedimentary rock is formed from the remains of eroded mountains, including sand, clay, rock, salts, and animal remains. Limestone is a type of sedimentary rock.

species (SPEE-sheez) A species is a kind of plant or animal. Caribou and reindeer are the same species.

steppes (STEPS) Steppes are sweeping grasslands. Grasses in the steppes can grow more than 4 feet (1.2 m) high.

taiga (TIE-guh) Taiga is thick forestland. In the Urals, the taiga lies between the steppe and the tundra.

tributaries (TRIB-yuh-ter-eez) Tributaries are rivers that feed into a larger river. The Tobol and Iset are tributaries of the Ob River.

tundra (TUHN-druh) Tundra is a treeless ecosystem in the far north or on the upper portion of mountains. Tundra supports fewer animals or plants than forested ecosystems.

A Urals Almanac

Extent

Length: 1,500 miles (2,400 km)

Width: 20 to 200 miles (32 to 322 km)

Continent: The dividing line between Europe and Asia

Countries: Kazakhstan and Russia

Major ranges: Middle, Northern, Polar, and Southern

Major rivers: Belaya, Kama, Ob, Pechora, Sakmara, Servernaya, Ural, and Vishera

Major lakes: Bolshoye Shchuchye, Itkul, Tavatuy, Turgoyak, and Uvildy

Major cities: Chelyabinsk, Krasnoturinsk, Magnitogorsk, Nizhniy Tagil, Severouralsk, and Yekaterinburg (Russia)

Major languages: Bashkiri, Kazakh, Tatar, and Russian

High peaks:

Gora Narodnaya	6,214 feet	(1,894 m)
Karpinsk	6,161 feet	(1,878 m)
Manaraga	5,971 feet	(1,820 m)
Zatshita	5,932 feet	(1,808 m)
Sverdlova	5,906 feet	(1,800 m)

Parks and preserves: Arkaim, Ilmenski, Pechora-Ilych, Shulgan-Tash, and Yugyd-Va

Natural resources: Asbestos, coal, copper, granite, gypsum, iron ore, jasper, manganese, natural gas, oil, and salt

Native birds: Black woodpeckers, capercaillies, carrion crows, ducks, eagles, falcons, geese, grouses, kestrels, and owls

Native mammals: Arctic foxes, badgers, brown bears, caribou, dormice, elks, ermines, foxes, ground squirrels, hares, hedgehogs, jerboas, lemmings, martens, mice, moose, otters, rats, sables, Siberian chipmunks, Siberian weasels, shrews, susliks, and voles

Native reptiles: Adders and grass snakes

Native plants: Arctic poppies, aspens, bedstraw, birches, fireweeds, larches, lichens, lindens, lupines, marsh violets, mosses, oaks, oxeye daisies, pines, rosebays, sedges, Siberian cedars, and wild grasses

The Urals in the News

250 million years ago	The European and Asian Plates collide to form the Ural Mountains.
300,000 years ago	Early humans live in Siberia.
15,000 years ago	Early humans draw pictures of animals on the walls of Kap Cave.
8000 B.C.	People begin to farm on the slopes and steppes of the Urals.
A.D. 1100s	Russian fur traders and colonists move into the Ural Mountains.
1200s	People in the Southern Urals first collect honey from Burzyan honeybees.
1598	Verkhoturye becomes the first real city in the Urals.
1630s	The first ironworks is established in the Urals.
1723	The city of Yekaterinburg is founded.
1917	A revolution installs a communist government in Russia.
1924	Russia joins with other nations in eastern Europe and central Asia to form a new nation called the Soviet Union.
1957	A nuclear accident leaks radiation near Chelyabinsk.
1990	The Shulgan-Tash Preserve is established in the Southern Urals.
1991	The Soviet Union breaks apart; Russia and Kazakhstan become independent countries.
1994	Yugyd-Va National Park is established.

How to Learn More about the Urals

At The Library

NONFICTION

Guek-Cheng, Pang. *Kazakhstan.* Tarrytown, N.Y: Benchmark Books, 2001.

Murrel, Kathleen Berton. *Eyewitness: Russia.* New York: DK Publishing, 2000.

Nickles, Greg. *Russia: The People.* Toronto: Crabtree Press, 2000.

Robson, Pam. *Mountains and Our Moving Earth.* Providence, R.I.: Copper Beech Books, 2001.

Wilson, Neil. *Russia.* Austin, Tex.: Raintree/Steck Vaughn, 2000.

FICTION

Ransome, Arthur. *Favorite Russian Fairy Tales.* Mineola, N.Y.: Dover Publications, 1995.

On the Web

VISIT OUR HOME PAGE FOR LOTS OF LINKS ABOUT THE URALS:

http://www.childsworld.com/links.html

Note to Parents, Teachers, and Librarians: We routinely verify our Web links to make sure they're safe, active sites—so encourage your readers to check them out!

Places to Contact

CONSULATE OF THE REPUBLIC OF KAZAKHSTAN

866 UN Plaza

Suite 586A

New York, NY 10017

212/888-3024

RUSSIAN NATIONAL GROUP

130 West 42nd Street

Suite 412

New York, NY 10036

877/221-7120

Index

About the Author

Barbara A. Somervill is the author of many books for children. She loves learning and sees every writing project as a chance to learn new information or gain a new understanding. Somervill grew up in New York State, but she has also lived in Toronto, Canada; Canberra, Australia; California; and South Carolina. She currently lives with her husband in Simpsonville, South Carolina.